THE REAL SILVER DOLLAR

FOREWORD by Les Brown

written by billionaire brown

Sale of this book without a front cover may be unauthorized. If this book is coverless, it may have been reported to the publisher as "unsold or destroyed" and neither the author nor the publisher may have received payment for it.

Published by New Money Publishing Group
Copyright by Demetrius Brown

All rights reserved.

All rights reserved and transferred June, 2012, to rich before thirty Company

Published in the United States by rich before thirty Books, an imprint of The New Money Publishing Group, a division of New Money, Inc.,
New Jersey.

Edited by Frowns To Smiles Editing...

www.richbeforethirty.com

Manufactured in the United States of America

This book is dedicated to Sabali, Hadiya, Londyn, Zhariya, and Mateo. I love you and look forward to your growth as we grow old together!

Love Uncle Dee

Les Brown Foreword

We are living in a time where millions of people are losing their jobs, their retirement, and are desperately looking for ways to secure their future. It has been said that recession restores resourcefulness. There are few people who realize that now is the time for us to look within to live from the place of power, creativity and gratitude. Demetrius Brown, better known by Billionaire Brown gives us "A Real Silver Dollar". A focus book that takes you on an exciting path of insight and reflection. In a world where many people have forgotten how to believe, let alone live their dreams, Brown addresses many truths that will free those who are bound by the disappointment of life. I am a firm-believer that you don't get in life what you want, you get in life what you are. This book is built upon two principles from my favorite book, "thou shalt decree a thing and it will be established unto you" and "we must call forth those things that be not as though they were." The Real Silver Dollar is designed to encourage you to discover the billionaire in you. By deliberately working on yourself, you will transform your mindset and expand your skills. You will build a community of wealthy, collaborative, achievement-driven relationships that will inspire you to create extraordinary wealth. Billionaire Brown equips you with the tools to have a larger vision for your life. In A Real Silver Dollar, Brown highlights the strengths and weaknesses of our current society made up of those who are thinkers and those who aren't. So where do you stand? Are you ready to unlock the greatness within you? I encourage you to open up your eyes and embrace the dreams waiting to manifest in your life. Use this book as a guide to accompany you on your journey of success. You will be given the inspiration you need to live full and die empty. It's time to give it your all and Live Your Dreams! Your greatness awaits you.

Les Brown

Table Of Contents

Chapter I. Believe

Chapter II. Preparation

Chapter III. Slow Motion is Better Than No Motion

Chapter IV. Focus

Chapter V. Waste Money. Don't Waste Time

Chapter VI. Consistency

Chapter VII. Knowledge is Old News

Chapter VII. Coach or Die

Chapter IX. Focus is More Than Paying Close Attention

Chapter X. Bury The Ego

Chapter XI. Brand The Legacy

Chapter XII. Only Hear Action

Chapter XIII. Let Your Actions Explain What You Say

Just because everything is different doesn't mean anything has changed

Introduction To The Real Silver Dollar

My name is Demetrius Brown and I am a money magnet. Money goes through near death obstacles to find its way to me. Lets move forward and go behind the scenes of the highly anticipated book everyone has been waiting for, The Real Silver Dollar. The purpose of this book is for all the regular people, like me, that are open for change.

Which brings us to why I named the book The Real Silver Dollar? The name, "The Real Silver Dollar", has two meanings: (1) The Silver Dollar Coin is the highest form of change that equals one American dollar. (2) All who lives by the Silver Dollar thinking are committed to reaching the highest form of change in their lives.

Lastly, before we open up the Real Silver Dollar way of thinking I must say rich before thirty is not an age, it's an Attitude! In the arena of network marketing when most people say rich before thirty most people realize we mean rich before the next 30 months, rich before the next 30 weeks, rich before the next 30 meetings you attend, etc. Results have always been a direct reflection of the effort we put into a particular thing. If you desire faster results, then simply increase your efforts. It's now time to move forward with The Real Silver Dollar! There's an old saying, that you can lead a horse to water but you can't make him drink or you can lead a person to knowledge but you can't make them think. Let's think about that horse that you have led to water and has been refusing to drink for years. The million dollar question is are you open to pouring salt down the horses throat to make him thirsty? If your answer is yes and you prefer thirst rather than force you will love this book because it was not written with the intent to change your thinking. It was written with the intent to remind you that change is the only thing that is constant in our lives. So lets embrace it with open arms!!

Chapter I

Believe

      I will always remember the day I knew greatness was due to self development and BELIEF. A couple years ago I received a random call from the legend Les Brown in the middle of the night. When I received the call at that moment I knew for sure it was a friend playing a trick on me, as my friends and I always do. I picked up my cell phone and he says, "Hello may I speak with the Great Demetrius Brown?" I said, Yes this is he." He goes to say "I first want to explain my not being in your life as I was in your sister" he also mentioned. "First I want to let you know I am sorry for being backed up on child support(jokingly)"..which is a inside joke that we have because of us being family friends and having the same last name Brown. He says "that I want to be your personal mentor and foreword your first book." At this point in the conversation I realized it was really him. Surprised and speechless I listened to everything he had to say to me as I stepped into my students role of taking advantage and being prepared for the opportunity. It was around 1 am in the morning and after he speaks to me he says, "I would like for you to come back to New York City in the morning at 8am." He requested that I join my mother, my grandmother, and him for a birthday dinner he arranged for my grandmothers 70th birthday in New York City. I quickly recognized the opportunity in front of me and completely forgot about the fact that I was extremely exhausted from the drive from New York City to Maryland hours before and instead I confidently

said "Yes I will drive back!" I still believe this may have been the best decision I have made in my life at that point. I share this with you because for me it exemplifies the power of BELIEF. Check out the cover of this book. It has a only one foreword and that is from the living legend everybody loves Mamie Browns Baby Boy Les Brown.

So do you BELIEVE?

    If yes then continue reading this book. If you do NOT BELIEVE that YOU can change, Google "Hebrew Chapter 11 verse 1". Now when you BELIEVE and perform as if, you begin to tap into the famous Triple A's...

* Always

* Abundance

* Awareness

$ALWAYS$

Thanks to Les Brown, I now ALWAYS follow up with clients, friends, and family. This is important to me because if I don't, I realized that someone or something else will. I have committed to being that someone. Imagine something getting in the way of your family because of you not having the priority of ALWAYS. Have you realized that anything besides the attitude of ALWAYS throughout history has led many people to the misuse of Drugs, television, food, alcohol, mediocrity, negative people.etc

Right now are you ALWAYS on top of the best that's out there? Or right now are you ALWAYS okay with mediocrity?

Silver Dollar thinkers are ALWAYS in Front of the room or the first individuals in the front. Silver Dollar thinkers ALWAYS create time for those in need. Have you ever told someone that you know that you didn't have the time to meet, listen, or talk and the next thing you know you're watching television, chatting with your friends, or doing something unproductive?

ALWAYS search for ways to do the little things that you can to make a difference in someone's life.

Silver Dollar thinkers ALWAYS have a mentor in every area of their lives. (Proverbs 10:17) reads " He who keeps instruction is in the way of life, But he who refuses correction goes astray." If life permits, search for a mentor or an accountability coach in every aspect of your life. The misconception is having a coach is not necessary for professionals and that only amateurs need a coach. History has consistently shown that it is exactly the opposite. Professionals ALWAYS have a mentor and Amateurs never do.

Have you ever procrastinated on doing something that was going to benefit your career or business and did not because of the lack of information, will, or drive?

ALWAYS have access to a coach…To not have a coach is to simply not perform at 100%

$Abundance$

Just a few days ago I was skimming through my mail separating letters from checks, bills from miscellaneous. As I came to the bills pile of my mail. One of the bills I came across was from an old cable bill I let slip into collections. I opened this bill like all the others although something that was drastically different about this one. This bill had a check in the amount of $23.51 inside! I agree this is not a large check, however ask yourself how much was the check in the last bill that you opened?

Do you think ABUNDANCE?

Do the top 5 people that you communicate with think with abundance? Or is the thought of ABUNDANCE lacking in your life?

So the childhood dreams of the 5 bedroom homes with the horses in the backyard, to become president of the United States of America, first female to travel to space, not only can come true with an

ABUNDANT state of mind but WILL come true. Let's think ABUNDANTLY for a moment. As a family we have seen the power of someone's ABUNDANT belief in the power of God. In my lifetime I have been blessed to see my father Kenny Watkins overcome throat cancer without skipping a single beat. The same breathe my father was diagnosed with cancer was the same breathe he was cured of cancer because of his ABUNDANT belief in a higher power. I have also seen abundant thinking play in our lives financially.

I will forever remember the movie "Lion King" when Mufasa is conversing with his son Simba and Mufasa takes his son to the edge of land and says, "Everything the light touches is our Kingdom". I admire this advice by Mufasa to his son Simba because it's true beyond measure. Everything in Life is available for us to take advantage of.

ABUNDANCE is something that comes thru belief in always getting more out of life, not through focusing on what we have already. Silver Dollar thinkers are individuals whom think ABUNDANTLY and are very supportive to all whom they come in contact with. To think ABUNDANTLY you never have time for small distractions. Why?

Because Silver Dollar thinkers are constantly searching for more, Silver Dollar thinkers are not sold. They are not talking about yesterday because if what you did YESTERDAY seems great, then you clearly didn't do anything today...

ABUNDANCE gives individuals the ability to give more, outside of themselves and their families. In fact ABUNDANT givers contribute hundreds and sometimes thousands of hours of their personal time giving back to communities around the world. Financially they give sometimes billions of dollars to just one cause.

Moving forward towards your Silver Dollar thinking you must clearly understand the gray area between abundance and greed. The best way I can describe Greed is by sharing a true story that was told to me by a gentlemen several months back.

He said, "There was a wealthy guy in Belize fishing in Fuji. There was a gentleman who saw the wealthy gentlemen fishing for a family of six. He caught seven fish and threw one back. When he threw the one fish back the other gentlemen said, "why did you throw that one back?" The wealthy gentlemen said "If I don't take more than I need this sea will always supply me with food for my family. If I take more than I need, I will be just like you needing money. "Abundance vs. Greed"

$Awareness$

In my opinion there are too many people telling people to do what they're not doing...Researchers have found that we have over 60,000 thoughts daily. On a scale from 1-10 with 1 being the worst and 10 being great...what number would you rank your sense of AWARENESS? Anyone who says you're a 10. I applaud your ability to believe your AWARE of all things both good and bad that comes at you every day. I warn you that there's a world out there seeking to be the first to bring your AWARENESS down. What if you thought your AWARENESS was perfect? And it wasn't?

Silver Dollar thinkers know there are 3 benefits of Good AWARENESS...

(1) AWARENESS gives you time to improve and apply massive action..(MOVE FAST BUT SLOW DOWN).

(2) AWARENESS allows you to realize when to step back and gracefully walk away

(3) AWARENESS puts you in position to be still and observe the situation....

AWARENESS is definitely like a muscle whereas it must be tested regularly to increase towards getting better and stronger. Let's continue to think of AWARENESS as we see the Street Lights. With street lights we have a Red light, we have a Yellow light, and we have a Green light. The green light represents the birth of a new idea or a concept. This is the most sensitive stage of getting anything started that's worthwhile.

The yellow light represents the feedback that the universe provides us for our efforts. The red light is the final results. Like on the highways whether public transportation or driving we can all agree that you never pull up to the same light. Green lights are what most of the world usually drive up to which are the potential possibilities that a single idea could have so when you reach the green light Go Go Go! Yellow lights create a 3rd party involvement which naturally causes us to slow down. One of two things occur when driving up to a yellow light

(1) Continue to drive thru which is to ignore the feedback of the 3rd party and keep going or

(2) Slow down and wait for the red light which is to digest the loss and see what has just happened. Red lights are where the results are and at that point we must STOP and analyze. Then decide if you are going to use the results to make you stronger or will the results wipe your idea out completely. The great news is that Silver Dollar thinkers know that red lights don't stay red forever. Like we discovered earlier change is the only thing in life that is constant. So let's get the results and move on or fail forward. What is a business experience that you lost out on because the lack of AWARENESS ?

High $Expectations$ Break

What are your EXPECTATIONS out of life?

Do you EXPECT Victory or do you EXPECT to be a Victim?

When you volunteer your time and/or money are you EXPECTING something to come back?

When you give a compliment are you EXPECTING one back?

And the most popular, when you give are you waiting for a thank you?

    If so, did you do it for the purpose of adding value to that person or did you do it for the acknowledgement?

    EXPECTING great things is a distinct characteristic that all Silver Dollar thinkers obtain.

    As a child about 5 years old, the month leading up to Christmas I would make my famous and lengthy Christmas list full of every new toy, bicycle ,video game systems, and as many chocolate candies as I could. When Christmas day came I would open up all of my gifts and I never would realize I did not receive all of the things on the list. So I urge you to have high EXPECTATIONS, the memory of a child, and the ability to continuously move forward.

In December if a homeless man EXPECTS a jacket and instead receives a sweater should he EXPECT for more or should he from that day forward take what life gives him and be content with the sweater?

Honestly most of what I EXPECT from life I rarely receive the perfect fit. Although there is something special about EXPECTING a lot and getting most of it. As oppose to the individual who EXPECTS nothing and ALWAYS receives it.

I'm a Big Believer in Preparation, Planning, and Prospering!

Chapter II

Preparation

In achieving the highest form of change you must be well equipped for the opportunities that life gives you. My advice is to keep God first and keep good company. I recall studying the climbing of Mount Everest which is the highest point on earth man/woman can reach. Many courageous climbers attempt and fail the Mount Everest mission. I have found it very inspiring of these brave individuals. In my opinion without a doubt climbing Mount Everest is one of the most amazing experiences mankind can complete. During the climbing of Mount Everest, one rule that I have found to be interesting is that if you lose a glove climbing Everest you will literally lose your hands. The weather gets as cold as below forty degrees on average. Did you know eighty percent of fatalities happen on the way down from the climb and only twenty percent occur on the way up. Prior to my research I assumed that statistic to be the other way around so I searched more. What happens is the climbers in the eighty percent category of fatalities on the way down train themselves over and over "I am going to climb that Mount Everest and get to the top no matter what it takes. "You ever heard the saying be careful what you ask for?

Unfortunately, these climbers did make it to the top, and nothing more. Their mission was accomplished once they reached the top, they never ever PREPARED for the trip back down... Take

a few seconds and think on how you PREPARE yourself for the things that you do. Just the thoughts that you tell yourself can set you apart from succeeding or failing. You will find that the same goes with your favorite sports teams, large corporations, growing churches, and established universities around the world.

The sports team that wins the championship are coached on one thing only. (We are going to win this championship this year and nothing else). This concept is understood thoroughly from the owners, to the coaches, to the trainers, to the cheerleaders, and throughout the entire organization. Other teams are set on if we won 5 games last season we must win at least 6 games this year. We all have to be PREPARED for our greatness.

There is another interesting part about the climbing of Everest. The leader must decide the best time for the team to climb or not climb. The last part of the summit (top) of Everest is the timing your team lead gives you for getting from the bottom, to the top. The team lead must immediately research several vital things such as the weather, speed of winds, and temperature.

When the team lead says go, you do so with no questions or you must wait until another moment is safe, according to the team leads judgment.

That is equivalent to opportunities that cross our path every day. Lets reflect on just the past 30 days. I am sure that we have heard, saw, and/or had a gut feeling about something ,thought about it, and you think about it so much when you go back to the opportunity it's gone forever. 9 times out of 10 you have to wait again for the same opportunity to come back around again.

We must treat opportunities as what they are. Which is a chance of change and not a guaranteed plan. Lastly, always remember its better to be prepared without an opportunity than to have an opportunity and not be prepared.

(WHO CAN INCREASE THERE ABILITY TO PREPARE? ...ANYBODY CAN)

Chapter III

Slow Motion Is Better Than No Motion

Slow Motion is the next step towards transforming to the highest form of change (silver dollar). It is being highly aware of the benefits of the old saying slow motion is better than no motion.

I recall having an old friend that had a incredible idea to start a business in the marketing industry. He had the layouts for proposals, he had who was assigned to each specific job, and he even knew how they would need to go about executing the assignment. Even better he knew exactly how much this idea was going to be worth. He offered me a position in his company and also gave me a layout. The one thing that I noticed, which was not attractive, was he left everything open for change. To paint the picture more clearly everything from the name of the company could be changed. He was committed to changing it all until everyone he told it to was excited about it. Obviously, this will never happen because you can never please everybody. I remember the words of an editor and journalist by the name of Herbert Bayard who said, "it has been said I can't give you a surefire formula for success, but I can give you a formula for failure which is to try to please everybody all the time."

When he first presented me with the idea he had already changed the name once. I told him what I thought about this approach. He felt temporarily confident with that and left everything but the name to be open for change.

Well a couple weeks into this idea his team began to disappear one by one. So when I called him during that period I asked him if I can come in and speak to his team. He told me that his team was falling apart as far as their loyalty level to his business venture.

In return, that experience lead him to lose his desire to do the business based on the energy his people passed to him. I clearly remember that at his lowest point of his business idea I paused and realized how disloyal we can be as human beings.

To make him see the power of courage which is to overcome any obstacle, I asked him. Has he ever wanted something like a pair of shoes and while shopping with someone else, you like the shoe and are ready to purchase without a doubt until the friend you are shopping with says they don't like the shoe?

Chances are you will not buy it. If there was more than one negative you might even request to speak to the manager and protest to have them taken off the shelf forever. (Jokingly).

On the other hand, if you go in a shoe store and fall in love with a particular shoe, try it on, and vision yourself in your favorite outfit! There is nothing and no one that can steer you,away from buying it.

      If you are easily broken, the people watching you will be the same. We must at least stay afloat with all that we do as if were walking a tight rope. There will be people that try to push us off, beat us down, and do all types of things to get us off that tight rope. It's not always intentional although people love to give input where there's a sign of doubt. So with any thought process leave no doubts to what you know and only to what you don't know.

Nobody has yet to do anything significant by accident. Everything significant has been done on purpose. DONT LIVE NOW...LIVE RIGHT NOW AND ALWAYS REMEMBER, Average IS JUST A WORD NOT A LIFESTYLE!!

(WHO CAN CREATE SLOW MOTION? ... ANYBODY CAN)

Chapter IV

Focus

I hate to lose MORE than I love to win.

In 3rd Grade I was in class and there was an annoying fly buzzing around the classroom. I felt that I could kill it. As an optimistic young fellow, I DECIDED to FOCUS and flick my pencil towards the fly about 10 feet away. To the entire class including teachers amazement I hit the target and killed the fly. Life changing experience for me although all of my classmates said it was LUCK.

I had already set in my mind that I was as great and talented as the greats I saw on television. Exposing the probabilities of life once you FOCUS on something.

Fresh out of graduating high school in 1998 I had a near death car accident. My 1988 Nissan Maxima flipped over 3 times and I ended up in a ditch upside down where I had to escape through the driver window. I got out of the smoking car beginning to catch fire and noticed that there was no blood, no scratches, no pain whatsoever. That day, I knew I was put here to share my story, I just had to find what that message was.

In 2006 I was on a plane flying from Texas to New Jersey for a business event, I was told I was a dead man with no pulse. After the plane was scheduled to make an emergency landing, a doctor on the plane was able to work with me and get me back to consciousness. I never made it to the hospital once we landed.

God has an interesting way of getting us back on track for what he puts us here for. Again I moved on in search of this message that I am here to share. The New King James Version Bible The Third Epistle of John verse 12 reads "Demetrius has a good testimony from all, and from the truth itself. And we also bear witness, and you know that our testimony is true."

I believe most people listen to me because I am passionate as they come and I believe there are two ways to approach becoming a successful person.

The most commonly used method in the world today is by force/power. The Silver Dollar method is by influence which most people say is the roadless traveled. I have noticed that both methods can get the job done.

Influence tends to last longer and can operate smoothly without you being present. Force/power is a form of energy that you have the ability of using while your alive in the physical. Influence is also something you have the ability of using while your alive and will be MOST recognized when you die in the physical. If you desire to lead through the reputation of your legacy, in due time you will be one of the key influential leaders in your network!

$ Who Are You With Break $

FRIENDS and BUDDIES must be identified immediately. Silver Dollar thinkers quickly identify the difference between Friends and Buddies by utilizing acronyms for them and I have listed the acronyms below:

F.R.I.E.N.D.S

(Fantastic.Reasons.I.Enjoy.Never. Dying. Soon)

Moving forward, pay close attention to the people you interact with most often and you will begin to notice all whom makes you feel good

B.U.D.D.I.E.S.

(Built.Upon.Day2Day.Instincts.Everyone.Suffers)

We all have buddies and there is a time and place for each of them. Moving forward, you will easily recognize who your buddies are in your life just because you have built a routine over a period of time.

Those who use force/power tend to have more B.U.D.D.I.E.S than F.R.I.E.N.D.S and those who use influence tend to have more F.R.I.E.N.D.S. than B.U.D.D.I.E.S.

Chapter V

Waste Money. Don't Waste Time

A person who aims at nothing is sure to hit it !

Before we go any further we must address some common ground which must be read in the beginning of these principles for two reasons:

(1) Time represents what all human beings have in common

(2) There's a clock ticking forward(Dreams) and there's a clock ticking backwards(Death)...bottom line the clock is ticking....

It has been asked to many what do all human beings have in common?

What I have come up with is we all share the same 24 hours in a day. There is no one that can get an extra five minutes or an extra hour. The only way you can get less than 24 hours in any day is when you pass away and go to live with our heavenly father. We all have the same 24 hours in a day.

What did you do with it?

When you continuously remember our proven business gurus like Bill Gates, Oprah Winfrey, and Donald Trump, they all have 24 hours. Not only do we share the same exact 24 hours but your 12 am is their 12 am, your noon is their noon, your midnight is their midnight....The most successful people share many things in common about their work ethics. The three that I have come to find that is most significant successful people sleep 4 - 6 hours a day, eat 3 times a day, and most importantly at least one hour of self development daily.

When I was seeking my greatness I was not sleeping 4 - 6 hours a day, I was not eating three times a day and I never had a mind strong enough to give myself any time for self improvement. The obvious difference is Silver Dollar thinkers work smarter and work harder. I recently read a powerful underrated book titled "Don't Sweat The Small Stuff ,Its All Small Stuff" written by Richard Carlson. This book convincingly gets the point across to not make problems that appear to be big, bigger as well as don't allow small things to appear bigger than they are as well. When I first read this book, I continued to ask myself, "what is big and what is small?" As I continued to read, I noticed my problem, the answer was so simple, it's all the same just don't sweat the small stuff....

Why?

Because it's all small stuff! Literally..... (Repossessions of house or automobile , divorces, health issues, bankruptcies) etc...

About 10 years ago the chances of becoming a millionaire were somewhere around 1 out of 1000 people and now the chances are 1 out of every 100 people are millionaires! Now we must realize those numbers are clearly not debt free millionaires, but definitely people who are bringing in a million dollars a year.

So evaluate your days and ask yourself how many times do you say you are always busy? How many of us are doing so much we don't have the time to do the things we REALLY want to do?

So through reading, meditating, and hanging around millionaires I came to a conclusion, my 24 hours is the only thing that I have in common with the most successful business people on this planet. So I will use it much more wisely and productively.

I have followed the tips of my mentor Les Brown and have mastered working smarter and working harder. This is the first step of evaluating your journey to success which is a small piece of obtaining the SILVER DOLLAR thought process.

So the next time we say we are being busy we must really mean it... (WHO CAN BE MORE AWARE OF THE VALUE OF TIME? ANYBODY CAN)

THE REAL SILVER DOLLAR

Chapter VI
CONSISTENCY

CONSISTENCY has been particularly defined as an agreement or harmony of parts or features to one another or a whole also the ability to be asserted together without contradiction. I believe that CONSISTENCY is a very critical characteristic that all Silver Dollar leaders must tap into. I support this strongly because it is when your mind, heart, body, and actions are in alignment when your consistency will prevail. This "Silver Dollar" characteristic I believe we must create goes back to elementary school.

Lets reflect on elementary school for a moment. When your primary teacher was absent and a substitute filled in, you probably acted slightly different then when the teacher was there. Whether that means acting up, misbehaving, or not learning anything the substitute was trying to teach. Or, how about those days at work when your supervisor or manager is out for the day. Are you as productive as normal or is that looked at like a relaxed day.........

Well here's the truth about it, greatness in life is not so much the things we do, but the consistence in which we do it. The act of a football player playing the game is simple, the act of a doctor performing surgery is simple, and the act of you going to work every day is simple. It is the CONSISTENCY and passion that we do it through all of the problems we have going on in our lives. By accomplishing the power of the "silver dollar thinking " you will understand that we all have the same problems, family, work, health, life. How you continue in what you do determines our greatness.

As you are approaching "Silver Dollar" status do everything to your best ability and do not hold anything back with the common excuses of life many of us are plagued with.

(WHO CAN Become more CONSISTENT?... ANYBODY CAN)

Chapter VII

KNOWLEDGE Is Old News

Knowledge is Knowing, Wisdom is Doing !

Are you applying all that you already KNOW? Do you ever find yourself with more information than results?

In the area of applying, I simply follow a method that I heard from the great philosopher Jim Rohn who says, "We must Study, Practice, and Teach." I value this philosophy because when utilized your life will never become stagnant.

To study is to be engaged in learning enough to comprehend the how-to. Once you comprehend the how to, you practice what you know. When your practice doesn't meet your EXPECTATIONS do it until it does. When it does meet your EXPECTATIONS you can now, and ONLY now, teach to others.

BEWARE of the amateur with the expert accent...

BEWARE of the people who have more ideas than production...

BEWARE of Excuses..

BEWARE of Negative Thinkers...

BEWARE of Success without Hard Work..

BEWARE of Small Thinking...

BEWARE of Opportunities...

BEWARE of Low Self Esteem...

BEWARE...

Silver Dollar thinkers understand that KNOWLEDGE is KNOWING and Wisdom is doing!

Chapter VIII

Coach Or Die

What requirements does your COACH ask of you? Do you need a COACH?

A COACH is necessary, mainly to keep you accountable on the goals that you set for yourselves. A COACH is there to celebrate when you succeed and to redirect you when you fail. Identify your COACH and give them permission to engage in guiding you towards better results. This prepares your COACH to begin logging 2 common things to your daily activities. What you did and also what you did not do.

Your COACH is not designed to nurture you and accept any excuses for your lack of production. Clear the separation from friend and COACH. I believe EVERYONE can use a COACH to become more.

$ Network Marketing Break $

Network marketing is the only industry out there that an individual can never be perfect. Network marketing is an ongoing growth experience anyone can do if they have the will to stay.

Do you ever feel UNDERPAID? Are you okay with having to REQUEST time off? Do you enjoy being scheduled, or told when to take a break, and when to be back from that break? Do you enjoy only having the ability to work when your work-shift starts till when your work-shift is over?

If your answer is no to more than 1 of these questions I highly recommend to find a network marketing company that best fits your liking immediately. In this industry don't procrastinate on taking action or lack thereof because anybody can, you just have to believe!!

Two Sure Ways to create cash flow in network marketing.

(1) Create your story...

I began network marketing as a favor of my mother Lorene Brown-Watkins who is the #5 income earner of a well known Affordable Healthcare Benefit Company. I only knew 2 things about the home based industry at that time.

(A) Donald Trump and Warren Buffet not only have their own network marketing companies but constantly say this industry is where average people can create wealth.

(B) Huge Tax Write-offs..That was all that I needed to hear on top of the fact that I was way under thirty years old and I was fed up with exchanging TIME for DOLLARS.

I was in position for time freedom so I began this journey. I quickly realized that I worked harder on my job than I did for myself. I quit the same network marketing company about 15 times. Although I was quitting and returning, which can only happen in this industry, I realized the "open door policy". Events/Briefings I attended around the country showcased a slew of amazing rags to riches stories. One story I will never forget is about a struggling gentlemen out of Dallas,Texas who joined our company by collecting soda cans and bottles to receive a nickel for each can to invest to get started. Today that same gentlemen has reached the top of our company which again showed me that yes, in network marketing "Anybody Can" you just have to believe.

I have been the big fish in small pond for most of my life. I have always been around great people, old and new acquaintances of mine that have both instilled and strengthened my Daily Disciplines. Burning Desire is something special that most do not have, but in this industry most are constantly pursuing. Individuals who have a burning desire believe if you what you did yesterday is big that means you haven't done anything today. When creating your story we must know like my mother always said to us "everything is a part of your story". When we look at a gravesite we see many things although to me the #1 thing I see is the dash, the time between the born day and the last day.

What did we do with the time we were given here on this earth? Who did we help? Who did we bring value to?

The dash is the only thing that we remember about individuals once they leave in the physical. We have come to find that those who have completed a lot in that dash are people whom have contributed a great deal to the universe and living with the intent to live forever.

Studies show that 70% of the people that go to a funeral do not go to the burial if it's raining outside. Those who have a burning desire have contributed so much to life that there true accomplishments cannot be measured until 12 months after there buried. It has been proven that Michael Jackson's empire is worth more now than when he was living!

Whose spirit can live forever? ANYBODY CAN....

(2).I recommend to anyone seeking to be successful in network marketing to PLUG INTO THE SYSTEM. Plugging into THE system NOT Plugging into A system. I believe We all do 1 of 3 things when exposed to a system:

Destroy THE System

Create A System

Use THE System

I have done all 3 and I find that Using THE System is most profitable for the majority. Using THE System is self explanatory although there are NO EXCEPTIONS. For example the State of New Jersey has a system that says you need a driver's license, registration, and insurance to operate a vehicle. The state system goes a step further and says if you don't have all of their requirements you will be penalized with a ticket.

In network marketing because it's considered volunteer efforts you can't get a ticket or penalized for not using the system, but rest assure you will not be getting paid.

Next thing you can do with a system is you can Destroy THE System. In my network marketing career I have traveled the road of Destroying THE System not so often.

Destroying THE System is not FUN nor PROFITABLE. For that reason many don't choose to stick with it for too long. This happens ONLY once you are aware of THE system. This is when you convince yourself, I don't need a license, registration, and insurance to drive. When you are not Using THE System you are fully aware. Although you truly believe you can be the exception to the rule. Some say this stage is denial. So now you put yourself and your family in DOUBLE TROUBLE. When you are not Using THE System and your expecting the results that come with Using THE System.

Lastly, Creating A System.

 This is the 2nd most popular stage I remained at. This stage appears to be very similar if not the same exact stage as Destroying THE System but far off. When Creating A System you are clearly saying I am larger than HISTORY. Creating A System is the easiest way to fail happily. Imagine one who gets pulled over by a police officer while driving and the officer says,"License, insurance, and registration." The driver responds confidently, "I don't need my license, insurance, and registration. I am going to give you my Master-Card, my passport, and this receipt from Macy's. Obviously this driver is in for a long day and a pile of tickets to go along with it. The beauty of Creating A System is it doesn't give or get feedback right away. Creating A System gives the ability to be unlimited, to feel in command, and to feel growth.

In network marketing people will do 150% of what you do wrong and 50% of what you do right. The worst part of what I found was that while I was Creating A System, so was everyone on my team which led to no checks and most importantly no duplication.

How do you eat a cake? One bite at a time. No matter if it's the best cake you ever tasted in your life you can only eat it one bite at a time.

Massive action gives us leverage to quickly see what works and what does not work. Massive action creates excitement and a huge following. So when we are taking massive action we must be strategic more than ever before. The industry is evolving so quickly. The technology, education and opportunities are changing by the minute.

If you're on fire people will come to see you burn. When you first get started with network marketing massive action overrules everything else.

Exposing your company to your friends and family members should be a breeze. I suggest friends and family for 3 leading reasons

> 1. It is just to let them know exactly what you have which secures your position to another networker exposing to them down the line!
>
> 2. To practice!
>
> 3. Friends/family as long as we just expose and not sell to them are a lifetime referral resource (Family is more inclined to HELP than to BUY)!

Remember when you expose and not sell, you not only have people listening out for people in need of what you have, you now have many friends/family you exposed to your company to as well! Now that ALL your friends/family are EXPOSED you can take massive action delivering your services or products to the general public while receiving great referrals from random contacts from time to time.

To date, I believe Les Brown sums up this industry the best . He simply says "TTP which stands for

Talk to People and if that doesn't work TTMP which stands for Talk to More People."

Massive Action + Massive Exposure = Massive Results. I have seen many sad stories of people within the same circle of network, in the same company, sponsored by different people all because a lack of massive action.

Do you have to be a Veteran to take massive action? Absolutely not... Anybody can... you just have to believe

Some of my favorite Network Marketing Legends

Dale Calvert

Jerry Clark

Dani Johnson

Art Williams

Big "Al" Tom Schreiter

I will forever have a special place in my business ventures for Network Marketing! Now enough of the Network Marketing Break, Back to Business

Hard Work Creates NEW MONEY !

Chapter IX

FOCUS Is More Than Paying Close Attention

FOCUS is another essential piece of transforming into your "Silver Dollar". Webster's dictionary defines FOCUS as a point of concentration. I want us to FOCUS for just another moment. Isn't it amazing how we FOCUS on things and more importantly the things that influence our FOCUS?

I have a business partner that always gets into debates with me on how great his cell phone is compared to mine. His argument is that he gets more minutes for a slightly less monthly premium and also his free nights begins 2 hours before mine, which means his nights start at 7pm ET. Since 1998 I have been with the same carrier for one reason and one reason only. The connection is always available. I have always been an analytical and logical person. If I have a car, I expect to be able to drive it at all times. If I have a phone, I expect to be able to use it at all times. A phone is to communicate at all times, not in some areas or some situations. For me, nothing else is more important than reception. Not minutes, not cameras, not family plans, and not day time or evening minutes. My intentions are not to benefit any cellular companies or speak badly on any either, but pick something that we can all relate to and show how we can subconsciously lose FOCUS.

Have you ever been a victim of picking out a carrier for one of many reasons mentioned?

My answer is yes and I hope I am not alone but for some reason or another we have committed to a phone carrier for really all the wrong reasons. Cause lets really ask ourselves what's better? Minute plans, family plans, roll over minutes, or communicating all the time?

I simply say if you have no service or your service is interrupted a little bit too often you can't even use those other optional benefits. The good news is majority of the time we lose FOCUS it is not our intentions, it is through other options giving us that appearance to be more attractive at the time you make that decision. Through becoming a

"Silver Dollar" you must FOCUS long term and bring out the binoculars. Not short term seeing with just your own eyes. Short term will always stray you away from what you need because when you ask yourself about a decision right now your mind automatically goes on what is right for your current situation.

Have you ever received a bill in the mail, looked at it, see it's exactly what you remembered it to be and for some reason or another just didn't pay it?

But sure enough when you receive the 2nd notice you see the late fees and other fees they charge, you sure enough get that bill paid right away. It's almost as if we need and want the warning signs to come so we can handle what we need to. I've researched that when we witness warning signs there are usually 3 things we do:

First: Fix the problem immediately

Second: Give a temporary fix

Third: Not fix it all and just wait for the problem to end itself until it cannot be fixed and only replaced by force or no other options.

As a "Silver Dollar" we must continue to remember problems were made to be fixed and people were designed to be great. On the other hand there are some situations where unfortunately we don't receive warning signs like cancers, car accidents, and other things of fatal consequences. So let's keep an eye out for the signs that life does give to us. Granted we can't fix all of them although there's a lot that we can fix and don't.

Pay attention to the signs you will receive today?

The pursuit of achieving the status of a "Silver Dollar" is achievable! Procrastination has to be controlled to a comfort in your life because time is the one thing that we as humans can never get back.

Here's a story that I once heard that goes perfect with this. Once there was a man drowning in the ocean waiting for GOD to come save him. First a family, who was out fishing yelled to the man, "Are you ok? We can make room for you just hold on there." The drowning man waved the family off and yelled, "No worries, God will save me. Then, one hour later a coast guard came

by to save the man in his boat. The drowning man waved the coast guard off again and said, "It's okay GOD will save me." So time went on and the man drowned and went to heaven. When he got to heaven he asked GOD. "Why didn't you come to save me" and God said" I sent two people to come save you and you waved them away" There will never be a more ideal time to act on something you want to do than right now... Always remember to take heed of the signs in front of you and you must take advantage of opportunities for the experience and not for the wealth.

My mentor Les Brown beats this phrase into my head all of the time. "There is never a shortage of money, there is only a shortage of ideas. Remember, none of us will ever have the luxury of wasting time."

(WHO CAN GET BETTER AT PROCRASTINATING LESS? ANYBODY CAN)

Chapter X

Bury The EGO

EGO which is another characteristic that must be controlled before reaching "Silver Dollar" achievement. EGO is often talked about in conversation, although I just want to clear the definition to those that are unaware. EGO is defined as the one of three divisions of the psyche in psychoanalytic theory that serves as the organized conscious mediator between a person and a persons reality. For the past 31 years I thought I had an EGO. Seriously, I only thought that EGO was an over confidence that people acquire for one reason or another. I was never aware that it was a mediator between a person and whatever the reality of that person is. I once read a piece by Osho from "Beyond The Frontier Of The Mind." In this piece he says, "The difference of the 2 outside of the mediator is just like the difference between a real flower and a plastic flower. The EGO is a plastic flower- dead. It just looks like a flower, it is not a flower. You cannot really call it a flower.

Even jokingly to call it a flower is wrong, because a flower is something which, flowers. This plastic thing is just a thing, not flowering. It is dead. There is no life in it.

I recall going in for an interview at PNC Bank for a financial sales position after being self employed for a long time. When I went in to PNC Bank for my interview I realized that the corporate interview process has changed slightly. You must now hand in a resume, fill out a lot of paper work, log into their computer, and do another application a little repetitive to me but, a requirement by the government. Well, I had completed my part of the interview deal and was just patiently waiting to be called. While I was waiting an older gentlemen came in, handed his yellow envelope with his resume enclosed, did his paper work, and then the secretary set him up for the application on the computer. Not even 45 seconds into him filling out the application, he slouches in his chair like a little child in math class right before recess. He couldn't take this anymore so he calls for the secretary and says, "What do I look like filling this out taking up an hour of my time," he continued "My credentials are too great to have to do this." As I am sitting there wondering when he will stop to see me there in my nice 3 piece suit waiting to be seen. He looks at me, then the secretary, and tells her more aggressively to go in the back and tell the lady that was scheduled to interview him that he will not do this foolish procedure. The secretary says, "Okay and would you like to set up an appointment for another time?" He says "NO", she repeats? He says, NO again and says "go back there and tell the women now." She says okay. While the secretary is back there he turns to speak to me and says, "I don't know who they think I am but I am not filling out anything else" So as I feel my opportune moment to speak to this gentlemen I say, "Wow you are a vice president of what company?" He says, "Company XYZ." I said, "Oh okay so I guess you are here just for a position to do something on the side?" At this point I feel awesome because I am in control of a conversation with a disgruntled Vice President... He says, "NO they called me in regards to an executive position." At that very moment the secretary came back out and told the gentlemen that the lady in the back is busy but says that it is government required everyone must complete before the interview and asks him one last time would he like to go ahead and do the application he says, "No if my track record is not enough then I don't want to speak to you guys anyway..Goodbye."

To stay on topic of EGOS I definitely saw that gentlemen as a person that was looking for more than he currently had as a VP of company XYZ, but the EGO was definitely the rude gentlemen that did not want to follow any rules. On the other hand I quietly thought to myself what if his actions are what would be required and expected of an executive position. I mean his EGO was so convincing that I forgot he was there to hear about an opportunity for obviously something that interested him whether it was the position, the money, or the company. He was there for a interview but did not do it because of a procedure that everyone must do.   His EGO I believe was a huge turnoff for that company, simply for the fact that there was someone else there to hear him say that was not a qualities of a great leader.

The mastery of EGO in a way has us living two different lives:

(1) What we actually live

(2) That we want to live.

(WHO CAN HAVE MORE CONTROL OF THEIR EGO? ANYBODY CAN)

Chapter XI

Brand The Legacy

LIKE IT OR NOT
The Way You Live Is Your BRAND !

    The question is no longer what should you do when you're trying to figure something out. The question is picking out someone that you admire that is an expert in what you would like to do. Just think to yourself before you take action what would this person do?

    For me my example was people like Donald Trump, Bill Gates, and Les Brown. I would feel confident with anything that I would decide to do even if it was weird to most people I felt it was intelligent. I knew that was exactly what my mental, book, and audio experts would do in that particular situation.

I recall a situation where I got started with a company during the worse financial times in my life. At the end of my first interview I immediately knew I blew it out of the water demanding double of what I was earning at my previous job. Surprisingly, it was still a tough choice for me to make and I knew that if one of my mental experts were in my situation with the same opportunity they would have done exactly what I did and I achieved it!!

When I look at the success of Walmart I am forever reminded about its founder Sam Walton. Sam Walton's values are distinctly branded within Walmart, you would think he was still alive! Walmart strives as a company because they are duplicatable.

Have you noticed when you walk into a Walmart for the most part they look exactly alike? When current executives at Walmart think of how to expand or to handle a problem they don't think of what they would or should do. They think solely of what Sam Walton would do. Ladies and Gentlemen Sam Walton died April 5, 1992. Silver Dollar thinkers call that branding your legacy.

Before Sam died he was by far the wealthiest man in his family. Today his legacy is directly responsible for 6 Six of the Billionaires in this world. The Walton family Have More Wealth Than the Bottom 30 % of Americans. Silver Dollar thinkers no longer talk about getting rich they talk about becoming wealthy. Even if it was true that the rich are getting richer and the poor are getting poorer, are we just giving up on becoming wealthy? Let's continue to learn from individuals like Sam Walton who have created such a big legacy that he can provide well paying jobs for his entire family. Shoot for the moon and never be happy with the stars. Shoot for the moon and keep going back for the moon until you get there.

Silver Dollar Leaders understand that there is no (I) in team but there are three (I's) in responsibility. Growing up I always enjoyed watching all sports, especially the teams that were winning championships. I have noticed on championship teams that when there's only 2 minutes left in a ball game all role players continue to do well. In addition there's always one person that decides to go the extra mile and put the game in their hands "FOR THE TEAM". With 5 seconds left in a situation not every team player can take the last shot, catch the final pass, nail the final interview, or close the big deal. That one person that goes over and beyond in the closing seconds understands what it takes to be a Real Silver Dollar Leader. Again Silver Dollar thinkers are consistently reminded there may not be an I in team but there sure are three (I's) in responsibility. Adapt to maintaining a WINNING attitude as a lifestyle. Continue to let the leaders and players fall in place because that is Silver Dollar thinking!! Branding means more vacations, branding means giving when you don't have to give, branding is being the best mother/father, branding is a Lifestyle, branding is your Life. I urge you to brand your legacy starting immediately.

(WHO CAN BRAND THERE LEGACY ? ANYBODY CAN)

Chapter XII

Only Hear ACTION

Silver Dollar Leaders engage in massive ACTION towards an idea so they can receive the results of failure or achievement faster and then move on. Silver Dollar Leaders ONLY hear ACTION.

Silver Dollar leaders have realized that the world renown author "Ima Dugana" has played more than a big role in most people's lives. In our society Silver Dollar Leaders stay as far away from those people that often say IM GONNA DO THIS, IM GONNA DO THAT, I WANT TO DO THIS, I SHOULDA DONE THIS, I CAN DO THAT, AND I COULDA DONE THAT.

The voices around the world that constantly speak these words are not the leaders of families, friends, and companies. As the old saying goes "Everybody can tell you how to do it if they have never done it"... Silver Dollar Leaders understand that for people to hear them is only through their ACTIONS. Often leading from the front, rarely from the back and most of the time side by side!

Silver Dollar Leaders are always eager to attract a large following by what they stand for and what they speak about when people are listening.

(WHO CAN BEGIN TO LEAD FROM THE FRONT? ANYBODY CAN)

FAITH It Till You Make It !

Chapter XIII

Let Your Actions Explain What You Say

We Will Remember Your Actions way longer than We will remember Your Name

Don't SCREAM ….. Don't SCREAM

Silver Dollar Leaders have realized that throughout history people duplicate exactly what they're environment does. For many years I have seen many parents including in my family hear their children making a lot of noise and the parents scream out, "STOP SCREAMING!" If you have yet to notice, throughout time people will certainly do as they see you do more than they will do as you say. For the record I believe screaming may be useful in certain situations but not to teach someone to stop screaming.

(WHO CAN BEGIN TODAY LIVING WHAT THEY DO? ANYBODY CAN)

But Break

On this self-development never ending journey I have come to find that the word BUT is a lot more powerful than to transition what you are saying, writing, or thinking. If we were to look in the dictionary to find the definition of the word BUT, I truly believe that one of its meanings should mean zero. If you pause for a second and analyze your most recent conversations you will notice that everything that you say before you say the word BUT erases itself out and only pays attention to everything after the BUT.

I remember in my previous years I would say things like "I want to buy a new house BUT I have to get a better job first." Well I am here to tell you that studies show that before you get a house you must get a job first. The second part of that BUT statement is only important. The act of speaking that way is putting two opposites together to supposedly mean the same thing. I was amazed at this concept and how much we do not pay attention to what we say and more importantly the impact our words have on our actions. I have come to realize that one word can change an entire situation and in turn change your life.

My thoughts today as I am in my pursuit of the silver dollar thinking, I focus on using words of movement.

    Words of movement can be words like and, then, when, after, before. You will come to find out that you can not use these words and not have action. It is impossible. Something has to happen negative or positive. Words of movement provides action in the words you speak which in turn keeps you from a standstill. I once heard, "Many a false step was made by standing still," so avoid words like "BUT" that puts a instant halt to anything you are trying to project. Here you will see some examples that may appear funny but will not be to the person on the other end of your conversation.

"I love you baby!" BUT...........

I want to marry you! BUT............

I would help you with that…BUT……

I want to go to church this sunday.BUT……….

Even if you wanted to get creative and upgrade to an excuse specialist you can say I will do something and you will get the same exact result. Notice that no matter what you say after the word BUT will mean anything to the person you are speaking to. At the end of the day I suggest you continue to remembers your road to success is not a destination it is a journey.

***Speak It then Take Action..Speak It then Take Action. ***Speak It then Take Action

(WHO CAN BE MORE AWARE OF THE WORDS WE USE? ANYBODY CAN)

rich before thirty is not an age, IT'S AN ATTITUDE !

Continue to keep us in your Prayers........

We LOVE YOU ALL

Limited Edition Only

Three Questions He Asked

On October 16, 2012 I had an awesome session with my coach. The three questions that he asked me is what clearly made this session unlike any other. The first question my coach asked me was how did I attract 1 person to order 1000 books in one single order? The second question my coach asked me was how did I get sponsored for a 15 day mission trip to Thailand? The third question my coach asked me was what do i believe it takes for a individual to win?

My Answer to Question #1

The only answer I could honestly give to my coach on how I attracted 1 person to order 1000 books in one single order was "relationships". I went on to tell him that I was referred and scheduled to speak with someone about an idea I wanted to execute that had absolutely nothing to do with this book. My dear friend, all I know is that the new saying "the book is the new business card" is accurate.

Within the first two minutes of my scheduled appointment I was asked what do I do for a living. It had to be God because the first answer i spoke was that I am an author. Before I could mention everything else I do for a living they stopped me and only asked more questions about my book. They asked questions like the name of the book?, what is the book about?, who is the book written for?, who put foreword on the book?, and did I self publish the book? I answered each of there questions to the best of my ability as a new author and shortly after-that they visited our website www.richbeforethirty.com and downloaded The Real Silver Dollar book. Again I know God was involved in this entire process because the entire call that I was referred and scheduled to talk to them about to this day, has never been discussed. In fact, several days after that original call I received another call from them requesting to make a order for 1000 paperback books they wanted to have sent cross seas to several entrepreneurial organizations they are decision makers with. I once heard sharing is caring so the part of the story that I feel most proud about is the negotiating that needed to be done prior to the order being completed. Being that I am a new author and never received a large order like this I wanted to make it as easy as possible for the order to be filled quickly and smoothly for the customer. On the day of the official order I had remembered the vision of Henry Ford and what he has done for the automobile industry that most people in that time period were totally against. For the few that don't remember the automobiles in its early stages I will explain in brief. Automobiles were only available for the well off and the wealthy. Henry Ford wanted to change that way of living and he did, he figured out how to cut the cost drastically so that more people can buy this great new concept called automobiles. Most of you reading the paperback version of this have purchased this book at its retail value of $11.99. I am proud to say like Henry Ford, since they ordered 1000 books I cut the cost to only $8.99 per book with the intent solely to get this book to the masses. Many have said that I was foolish, although I remain strong with my belief that long term it was the best thing for the global presence of this book that many are now expecting to be a best seller. All in all I believe in Henry Fords model for growth of a great idea. Cut costs and deliver value!!

My Answer to Question #2

How did I get sponsored for a 15 day mission trip to Thailand? How I received this sponsorship is always a funny story to share. Several years ago I met a young lady named Gwendolyn Nicolas from the state of New York. Gwendolyn became a distributor on my team in one of the projects I currently am partnered with and from there we worked together building a nice team as well as building a lifetime relationship. As our friendship grew we discussed many things outside of the business project we were working on together. Among our many conversations I remember Gwendolyn sharing with me she has been part of 40 mission trips around the world helping people and spreading the gospel about Jesus Christ. As Gwen would talk about these mission trips i became more and more interested and eventually told her one day I would love to join her for this experience. Shortly after like most long lasting relationships Gwendolyn and i had parted ways on the project we worked on and went on our separate ways and didn't speak for a couple years. I would call Gwen from time to time and she would never pick up for whatever reason until she called me'. When she finally called me I was under the impression she was calling me to become a distributor on my team again to rebuild the project we once started. After a couple minutes of her talking not only did i realize how wrong I was about why she called me, but I also realized that even i struggle with thinking small sometimes. The lesson I learned is to never limit a good relationship to the origination of how the relationship was started. Gwendolyn is now 67 years old and values a relationship like very few I have met in my lifetime and I am grateful God

and my mother Lorene Brown- Watkins together connects her and I. So Gwen invited me to join her in Thailand for 15 days from October 16- October 31st. She originally mentioned it would be several thousand dollars and would require 100% of my attention while there on the mission. I had let her know I had just released my first book and could not invest my time, money, or anything else at this time. I proceeded to inform her that i would have to respectfully decline at to moment. Her excitement of hearing about The Real Silver Dollar not only caused her to pick up an autographed copy of the book but also she got more determined to figure out a way to get me sponsored and make it where i can still do everything necessary for my book while in Thailand as well. Before we hung up she promised she will make some phone calls and make this happen. Less than two weeks from that day Gwen called with full sponsorship from someone who I have not let yet although believes in all that I am doing. Flight, Hotel, Food, Translator, and even spending money. This for me was another confirmation to that saying " your book is the new business card", is true.

My Answer to Question #3

Out of all three questions I was asked this one was the most difficult for me to put in words for what I believe it takes for an individual to win? Winning occurs in every area of our lives from a child becoming potty trained to a young adult obtaining a promotion at the job. I said..

How to win ?

1st - We Must Think to Win

2nd - We Must Want to Win

3rd - We Must be Willing to Win

History Proves

Most people Think to Win!

Most people Want to Win!

Although most people are not willing to Win!

So

If you are prepared to Win ?

Your chance of winning is high!

If you have practiced and you are prepared to Win

Your chance of winning is higher!!

If you have practiced, your prepared, and expect to win your chances of winning are inevitable!!!

Winning is easy if your just willing to lose

prepare to win

Practice to win

Expect to win

Silver Dollar Thinkers Alumni

Henry Ford

Steve Jobs

Joel Osteen

Barack Obama

Warren Buffet

Mahatma Gandhi

Ray Kroc

Oprah Winfrey

Barbara Walters

Jay-Z

Derek Jeter

Russell Simmons

Larry King

Ben Carson

J.K. Rowling

Tupac Shakur

Kobe Bryant

Michael Jackson

Frank Sinatra

Stevie Wonder

Richard Pryor

Spike Lee

*Personal Disclosure: If what you did yesterday seems big, then you are not a silver dollar thinker. These individuals I listed above reflects in my opinion always in-tune of what MORE can be done daily to strengthen there craft. Again my opinion so there listed IN ORDER beginning with #1..

Special Thanks

Holy Bible

Lorene Brown-Watkins

David Sunflower Seeds

Uncle Rolando

Wilson Basketball

Robin Brown

Sprite

The City of Philadelphia

Sharpie

Lil Mikey

Kenny Watkins

Money Stacks

Square

Change In My Pocket

I-Tunes

Apple

Latasha Jones

Think and Grow Rich

Richest Man in Babylon

Casado Boys

rich before thirty fans!!

Stay Tuned For My Next Book Coming Jan 2013..." The CAPITALISTIC BUTTERFLY"

www.ingramcontent.com/pod-product-compliance
Lightning Source LLC
Chambersburg PA
CBHW080946170526
45158CB00008B/2386